The Best Day Ever

Hilton Head Island

written by Ellen Giordano

illustrated by Liz Beatty

Ellen Giordano

Ordering Information:
Quantity sales. Special discounts are available on quantity purchases by corporations,
associations, and others. For details, contact the publisher at **hiltonheadkidsbooks.com**.

ISBN 978-1-7923-9363-1

For Stella, Lila and Leo
and all the children who
love this island.

The sun is rising, a new day has begun.
We are ready for lots of Hilton Head Island fun!

It will be the best day ever; there's so much to do,
Many adventures are waiting for me and for you!

We head to the beach, a great place to begin,

To splash through the waves and go for a swim.

We build a sand castle; do whatever we like,
Fly a kite, look for shells, even go for a hike.

On to Coligny fountain, to splash with our feet,
We have a happy time with all the friends we meet.

At Celebration Park

there's a children's museum to enjoy,

Then we climb aboard the ship on the playground

and call out, 'Ahoy!'

South Beach is next, so many dolphins to see,
They cruise by the shore just to greet you and me.

It's up to the top of the lighthouse we go.
We see lots of boats in the harbor below.

We pass by a playground and stop for awhile,
Scamper onto the oak and walk single file.

With ponies to ride and animals to see,
Lawton Stables is a place we love to be.

In Sea Pines Forest Preserve, on bikes we ride.
We are searching for animals trying to hide.

We spy egrets and blue herons, for this is their home,
An alligator appears and we leave it alone.

We paddle our kayak, through a marsh on Broad Creek,
We see many creatures, it's adventure we seek.

We stop at a restaurant, for a basket of shrimp,
Fresh from the ocean, on this we won't skimp.

The Coastal Discovery Museum is a great place to explore,
The scavenger hunt and butterfly garden we simply adore.

As the sun starts to set on the island we love,
Bright colors astound from the sky up above.

Next it's to Shelter Cove Harbour we go,
To watch a spectacular fireworks show.